A ROAD MAP FOR

JOURNEY TO

NEWLAND

TRANSFORMATIONAL CHANGE

BILL POOLE

with DARYL HOLT

Illustrated by Andy Dorsett

Foreword by Kevin A. Henry

BICENTENNIAL
1807
WILEY
2007
BICENTENNIAL

Pfeiffer™

John Wiley & Sons, Inc.

Copyright © 2007 by John Wiley & Sons, Inc.

Published by Pfeiffer
An Imprint of Wiley
989 Market Street, San Francisco, CA 94103-1741
www.pfeiffer.com

Wiley Bicentennial Logo: Richard J. Pacifico
Interior Design: Gene Crofts

For additional copies/bulk purchases of this book in the U.S. please contact 800-274-4434.

Pfeiffer books and products are available through most bookstores. To contact Pfeiffer directly call our Customer Care Department within the U.S. at 800-274-4434, outside the U.S. at 317-572-3985, fax 317-572-4002, or visit www.pfeiffer.com.

Pfeiffer also publishes its books in a variety of electronic formats. Some content that appears in print may not be available in electronic books.

Library of Congress Cataloging-in-Publication Data
Poole, Bill.
    Journey to Newland: a road map for transformational change/Bill Poole with Daryl Holt; illustrated by Andy Dorsett; foreword by Kevin A. Henry.
        p. cm.
    ISBN 978-0-7879-9440-2 (pbk.)
    1. Organizational change. 2. Teams in the workplace. 3. Conflict management. 4. Animals—Fiction. 5. Survival skills—Fiction. I. Holt, Daryl. II. Title. III. Title: Road map for transformational change.
    HD58.8.P66 2007
    658.4'06—dc22   2007013370

Printed in the United States of America
Printing   10   9   8   7   6   5   4   3   2

This book is dedicated to

Bob Pettus and Jerry McKinney,

my mentors and friends.

Special thanks to

Kevin Henry and Kelly Jordan
for their vision and support

Bob Bruton and Dick and Lynda Jordan
at LifeLead International

Daryl Holt and Jason Renfroe
*for their creativity, technical expertise,
and moral support*

Greg Gray and Karen Gray
and the Gray Training Team in South Africa

Lisa Shannon and her team
at Pfeiffer, Wiley, and Jossey-Bass Publishing

My clients
who believe in these principles and verify them

Keith Moore
for his friendship and support all these years

My closest friends
(you know who you are)

My parents

CONTENTS

Contents

Contents

FOREWORD

I am indeed honored that Bill asked me to write the foreword for *Journey to Newland: A Road Map for Transformational Change.*

Bill has been a friend and inspiration to me for the past several years. I have admired his intellect, his creativity, and his perseverance to "stay the course" no matter how challenging the journey.

Ever since he came into my office at Coca-Cola Bottling Co. Consolidated and began discussing his vision for how to put principles and faith into practice in the workplace and in life, I have been struck by his passion and commitment to use his work as a platform to make a difference in the lives of others. As we chatted that day for several hours, I could envision myself, my employees, and even my family benefiting from the principles in Bill's work. The notion of change being transformational (moving from Oldland to Newland) is profound and requires a great deal of personal examination and conviction to navigate successfully.

I was attending church services recently, and the speaker was teaching about transition. He said, "We are all in one of three phases of transition at all times:

1. We are involved in crisis.
2. We are coming out of a crisis.
3. We are entering a crisis."

I'd never thought about it that way, but he was right. We as human beings are always in transition, whether as individuals or organizations. The speaker's perspective was that the good Lord is continually developing each of us, our character, our faith, and our spirit, through trials and tribulation. He routinely challenges our perspective, our beliefs, and our convictions. He is, in another word, transforming us in "real time" through our experiences.

I devoutly believe that those who are best equipped and humbled enough to be active learners and who have deep conviction in their values and faith principles are the ones most likely to successfully navigate transition and embrace transformation. I believe that *Journey to Newland* is a thoughtful body of work that lends itself to personal introspection in a way that brings clarity to what individuals and organizations stand for in their cultural contexts. Beyond helping one develop perspective, *Journey to Newland* provides real insights into how best to prepare for and eventually make the trip, ensuring the greatest likelihood of success.

I remember that first meeting as though it was yesterday. Bill shared his perspective on how to use the power of metaphor to educate and build personal and organizational capability. Who would have known that several years and lots of "blood, sweat, and tears" later, Bill's vision would become a reality?

We at Coca-Cola Bottling Co. Consolidated have been using the principles reflected in Bill's work to lead transformational change. I must also admit that I have put several of the principles into practice in my own home with my wife and two sons and when dealing with my own personal relationships. I am pleased to report that although we at Coca-Cola Bottling Co. Consolidated are not finished yet with our journey, I am confident that the best is yet to come as we move closer to Newland and all of the prosperity that awaits us there.

Enjoy the journey!

Kevin A. Henry

Senior Vice President
Chief Human Resources Officer
Coca-Cola Bottling Co. Consolidated
Charlotte, North Carolina

PREFACE

The *Journey to Newland* story grew out of necessity. At LifeLead International we produce content for personal, team, and organizational capability, and the vision for all that we do is "Building Lives and Leaders." *Journey to Newland* was conceived as a way to illustrate this vision and the processes that support it.

For several months I had been searching for a way to explain a complex transformational change process in simple terms to help our clients. One day I went to walk and think at Fort De Soto Beach near my home in Tampa, Florida. That day, as I watched the different animals gathering around the same water source for survival, *Journey to Newland* was born.

Since that time *Journey to Newland: A Road Map for Transformational Change* has grown rapidly and is being used to navigate change all over the world in many languages and cultures. As the concept matured, an array of materials and services that support the story have been developed, such as the *Journey to Newland* DVD movie, state-of-the-art teaching tool applications, facilitators' guides, participant notebooks, prework booklets, simulations, games, posters, certificates, internationally recognized assessments, facilitator and consultant certification, supplemental courses, consulting, and coaching. (See www.journeytonewland.com for more details.)

If you wish to delve deeper, contact us or the publisher, and we will gladly assist you. If not, enjoy the book; read it for your personal and professional development. Either way, we will have met our goal of "Building Lives and Leaders."

Bill Poole

CEO/President
LifeLead International
Tampa, Florida
www.lifeleadint.com

INTRODUCTION

Welcome to the journey . . .

It was a time when everyone seemed happy and content . . . until the day a dark wind arrived, carrying with it the bitter seeds of change. . . . Now the animals in Oldland are faced with the greatest of challenges: How will they leave the secure land they loved and find a new land of growth and opportunity? The strategy that Eagle implements with his Coalition made up of Owl, Lion, Dolphin, Ant, and others offers us a virtual *road map for transformational change.* In this symbolic story you will see how Eagle and his team develop leaders, overcome the Resistance, and value differences in order to find a *new land blooming with opportunity for all.*

But this is much more than a story. *Journey to Newland: A Road Map for Transformational*

Change is an animated life and business simulation that can help guide you, your team, or your organization onto a new path of growth and change.

This story was written to illustrate a complete process for transformational change that is based on more than twenty years of research, implementation, and consulting for some of the most successful companies in the world. Because I was dealing with international organizations, I was searching for a memorable methodology to articulate an intangible, complex process in tangible, simple terms that was true to experience, scalable in content, and culturally flexible and adaptable.

Journey to Newland provides a complete landscape of principles for transformational change. Effective principles remain the same regardless of any change in context. This story incorporates vital principles that the inhabitants employ throughout their journey. Look closely for the principles of leadership, integrity, responsibility, respect, learning, openness, trust, and cooperation throughout the pages. Try to spot them as a watermark on the landscape as you read.

Journey to Newland provides a scalable mountain of content for transformational change. This story allows you to scale to different levels by using a common language. And lack of a common, unifying language is one of the greatest barriers to transformational change.

If the mountain represents the full extent of the Journey as illustrated by the story, you can scale the content to whatever point of engagement you need: the executive team, middle managers, corporate office, branch offices, or employee orientation. It can be used for transformational change initiatives in business, education, nonprofit organizations, communities, local governments, and even nations.

The symbolic places in *Journey to Newland* were carefully chosen to mirror real-life situations. The Globaland map lays out a clear picture of when and how to leave Oldland; overcome the obstacles of Nostalgia Desert and Comfort Valley;

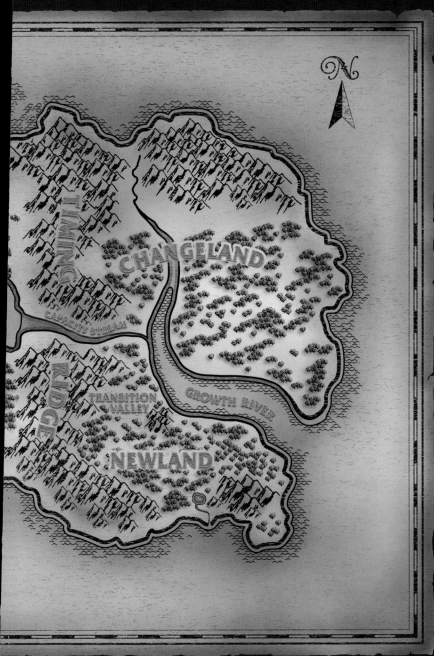

utilize the Meeting Place, Resource River, and the Grapevine; find Leverage Lake; cross Timing Ridge; widen Capacity Stream; navigate Growth River and Changeland; blaze through Transition Valley; and reap the opportunity in Newland.

The characters in the story demonstrate some basic responses to change, but they also reveal a deep study in human behavior and provide team and organizational capability awareness and intervention strategies. The Coalition and the Resistance are separated by their priorities and values, and each animal and their tendencies in each team can be compared with the others for more depth and awareness.

Journey to Newland provides a steady stream of practical skills for transformational change. The story constantly integrates the core capabilities of leading *change*, developing *leadership*, building *teams*, valuing *differences*, and optimizing *communication* (the "Big 5"). It also provides an illustration of how to successfully navigate the eight stages of successful transfor-

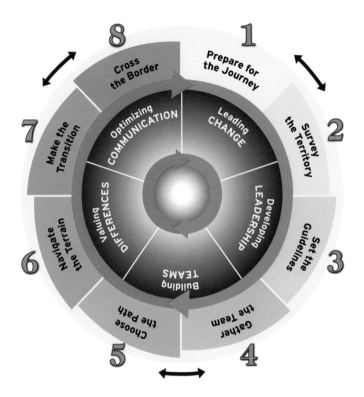

mational change. You can track these eight stages in the left-page headers of this Introduction and throughout the story.

Let the Journey to Newland begin!

Once, there was a place called Globaland, a distant continent where all creatures lived together. But it wasn't always that way. Long ago, the animals had lived in separate habitats. As time passed, desert animals began sharing green, fertile plains with inhabitants of the forest . . . sea creatures swam in sparkling, freshwater rivers with their friends from pond and stream . . . and life was good. Yet because of fear and uncertainty, the animals gathered only where life seemed predictable and safe. And so it was that vast areas of Globaland were left unexplored.

Until now . . .

A CHANGE IS COMING

This is the tale of the Great Change that fell over the land after the Seasons of Prosperity—a time when every creature in Globaland seemed happy and content. Most of the inhabitants of Globaland never even noticed the signs of the Great Change, but the watchful eyes of some were ever vigilant.

One bright and beautiful day Eagle was soaring over Oldland—a lush paradise that the creatures of Globaland called home. Eagle enjoyed

gazing at the blooming garden of trees and flowers within Comfort Valley and was ever thankful for the bounty of fresh, clear water known as Resource River that flowed throughout the land. Yet something troubled him.

Eagle flew south through Oldland, first following the river and then soaring past the Dinosaur Graveyard, before finally lighting on a branch at the edge of Nostalgia Desert. His eyes narrowed as he looked out upon the desert. Something was wrong. He stared intently, but whatever it was in the back of his mind would not reveal itself. With a laser look his eye focused on an old, gnarled tree, on which he saw a branch crack and tumble from its great height. Now he knew exactly what it was. It was something he had been declaring to others for quite some time: *the Great Change is coming.*

Eagle realized that Nostalgia Desert was expanding and was now encroaching upon Comfort Valley. Quickly he left his perch at the edge of the jungle and hurried back toward the north end of the valley. Eagle had seen signs of the Great Change in the past. He had observed the recent drought that led to barren trees, brittle soil, dusty air, and shallow waters. So he surveyed the land as he soared each day. But now reality faced him. The animals of Oldland must act, and act quickly, or they would surely die. Eagle flew to the home of his most trusted friend, Owl, with the hope that together they could discover what must be done.

DIVERSE CONSENSUS

It was still early in the morning when Owl left the comfort of her nest high in the trunk of the great tree where she had lived for many years.

Suddenly, a loud, bellowing voice broke the calm silence of the morning. "Owl!" yelled Eagle.

Startled, Owl opened her eyes wide. She was now well awake.

"Owl! It's happening, just as I said it would,"

Eagle cried as he landed on the branch of the great tree.

"What's happening?" asked Owl.

"The Great Change," said Eagle. "Nostalgia Desert is spreading eastward! I've seen it! Our life in Comfort Valley is in great danger. I tried to warn all of you!" he said, shaking his head. "Oh, why wouldn't anyone listen?"

"Oh, we were listening," corrected Owl. "It's just that some of us have a problem *believing*."

Owl was right. For months Eagle had warned of the coming crisis, but few believed him. The other Air Dwellers just *assumed* things would get better, so they kept their heads in the clouds flying higher and higher out of the dusty air.

The Tree Dwellers refused to leave the nests they had worked so hard to build. Stubbornly they remained, steadfast in the belief that the crisis would soon pass.

The Land Dwellers were content to graze and hunt in familiar fields—though food and water were becoming scarce.

The Soil Dwellers denied the reality of the brittle earth and just continued to dig . . . longer and deeper.

The Water Dwellers believed it was their fate to be trapped in the crowded, shallow river—thinking there was nothing that could be done. Eagle could clearly see that something must be done. But what?

"It pains me to say it," said Eagle, "but we must end our dependence on Oldland. If we don't, it will kill us." Looking down, Eagle continued, "It doesn't matter how good it's been to us in the past! Oh, Owl," he said after a pause, "I don't know what to do."

"Open your eyes," reassured Owl, "look into the hearts of everyone here, and you'll see we all have different perspectives and priorities—but we have one thing in common too—we all want to survive."

Owl continued to show Eagle that what he was missing was a team of diverse consensus, but Eagle did not react and maintained his grim look of despair. So Owl moved closer to Eagle and placed a wing on his shoulder to offer both comfort and wisdom. "There *are* others here who share your beliefs," she said. "Find them, but value the *differences* in each of them. Then they will truly believe.

"With the right team and a strong vision," continued Owl confidently, "anything is possible." Eagle smiled slightly, and Owl shuffled past him to return to her nest. "Now," she said, "go find your team, and together, I bet you can deal with anything—even the Great Change."

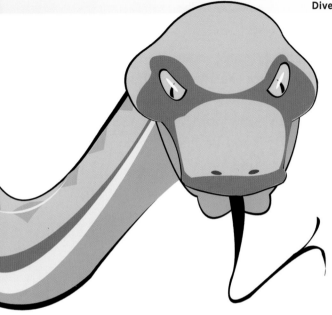

"You're right, old friend," replied Eagle with a sly smile, "and I know just where to start."

Owl glanced over her shoulder to see Eagle's grinning face. Realizing instantly that he wanted her to join the team, she countered, "Oh no! I've got to, uh . . ."

"C'mon!" challenged Eagle.

"But . . . but," she stammered.

Laughing, Eagle continued his campaign to convince Owl. Meanwhile, high above in the treetops, a shadowy figure was watching and hanging onto every word. Snake peered down at Eagle and Owl, and he hissed under his breath, "How interesssting."

A Team Emerges

Eagle knew it would be difficult to face the Great Change and convince the inhabitants to act, but Owl's advice made sense. So Eagle set out to form a team. He did not seek out others with different values, but he would strive to value the differences in each of the inhabitants just as Owl had suggested. He would form a team of diverse consensus, though he realized that the very differences he sought could ultimately be used for or against his cause.

Eagle and Owl set off together for the Meeting Place, where they would continue to recruit the team.

At the Meeting Place animals were already gathering to take part in their favorite morning rituals. Elephant and Hippo were bathing in the cool waters of Resource River while Dolphin teased them with unexpected splashes from her playful jumps. Turtles gathered at the riverbank and beavers engaged in animated conversation nearby.

In the midst of the activity, Chameleon scurried from one spot of the Meeting Place to another—stopping at each point to blend in with the nearest group and agree with whatever was being said. She finally settled next to Hyena, who was looking as grumpy as ever. When she attempted to assume Hyena's appearance and mimic her expression, Chameleon was met with a quick kick that sent her tumbling end over end into a small bush at the foot of Bear.

Bear was attempting to dig as much honey as possible out of a beehive while bees flew wildly around him. "Buzz off, bees!" he said with a

growl. This was, after all, *his* forest. At least it was in his mind.

There was a slight rustle of plants in the nearby Jungle. Bear paid it no heed. He knew what was coming. Off in the distance a hopping shadow could be seen, and with a final amazing leap, Rabbit burst forth from the Jungle. "Ta-daaaa!" Rabbit exclaimed as he landed in the clearing. "Honey of a day, huh, Bear?"

"Yeah," replied Bear, disinterested.

Having made his grand entrance, Rabbit went to feed his curiosity, hopping quickly toward his usual place to fill up on the new happenings: the Grapevine. Bees buzzed back and forth near the Grapevine, spreading their morning gossip and getting the latest "news" to be heard. Busy Bee was there too, and as soon as Rabbit spotted him, he quickly moved toward him.

"Hey, Bee!" said Rabbit, interrupting Busy Bee's humming. "What's the buzz?"

"Well, well, well . . . if it isn't Rabbit," said Bee.

"Heard anything new?" asked Rabbit.

Bee looked side to side to ensure that no one else was listening, hovered near Rabbit's ear, and whispered the latest gossip.

"You're kidding!" Rabbit gasped in dramatic disbelief.

"Oh yeah," said Bee with a raised eyebrow. "I got it from a really reliable source. Everybody's talkin' about it."

"Wow!" said Rabbit, shaking his head to clear the clutter. "Anybody seen Eagle?"

"I have," shot a voice from above. "I can't seem to shake him off my tail," said Eagle as he landed gently on the central stump. "Listen up, everyone!" he said, waiting for the other animals to gather around the stump as Owl landed gently on a rock behind Eagle. "Thank you."

As the animals continued to gather, Bear seized his opportunity. Quickly, his eyes darted back and forth as he peered to see if anyone else might speak up. Satisfied with the perceived lack of leadership, Bear cleared his throat loudly and raised a closed fist to his mouth to cover a cough.

"Ahem (cough)!" interrupted Bear. "What can we do for you, Eagle?"

"Well, Bear," replied Eagle, "it's more like what we can all do together."

Eagle continued by telling the others what he had seen that morning, and he shared his fears about the Great Change. He was held in lofty regard by his fellow Air Dwellers, so the other animals listened closely with quiet respect as Eagle laid out his plan to pull together a team of animals with one representative from each group—a team designed to look at the Great Change from every angle and propose a solution.

Looking over his shoulder, Eagle acknowledged Owl sitting on a large rock behind him. Owl, he told them, would represent the Tree Dwellers. Since Owl had the gift of flight, she could see the big picture almost as well as Eagle. She also lived in the trees, so she could look at the problem from both perspectives. And with her powers of observation, Owl was one of the wisest creatures in the land. She realized it was time to leave the safety of the trees and return to nesting later. She was indeed a very good choice.

Next, Eagle pointed toward the jungle and a large shadowy figure emerging from the underbrush. The other animals were curious, and their curiosity soon turned to awe as Lion, the King of the Jungle himself, emerged.

Eagle introduced Lion, a vision of strength, power, and royalty, to represent the Land Dwellers. Lion radiated humble confidence and trust, and he had earned the others' love and support because he never lorded his position over anyone. Lion knew he had their respect, but in these trying times, Lion's power to rule would depend on his willingness to *serve*. Once more, Eagle had chosen well, but Bear's pride was hurt.

Bear had spent years creating an intimidating image as a leader among the Land Dwellers. He was shocked that he was not chosen as the representative and insulted that Lion was picked for a role that he believed should be his and his alone. But most of the other animals gladly supported the choice of Lion, and Eagle smiled happily at their enthusiasm.

Eagle would represent the Air Dwellers. With his keen vision high in the sky, Eagle could see

the whole picture, and his intelligence, integrity, and character had earned the respect of almost every animal that knew him. Among the Air Dwellers, Eagle was the clear leader, but he believed this was the time to fly lower so that later, he could fly higher. But right now, he had a more lofty aim: completing the team.

"My friends," said Eagle, forming an inviting gesture with his wings, "Lion, Owl, and I will do everything in our power to determine the effects of the Great Change, but we need the help of everyone . . . including the Water Dwellers.

"Dolphin," he continued, "we need someone like you. How about it?"

All heads respectfully turned to look at Dolphin at the river's edge. Dolphin could rise smoothly out of the water at will, which gave her a broader perspective than most Water Dwellers. And though she was nice, she could skillfully hold her own with forceful creatures like Shark and Whale.

She accepted Eagle's invitation by clapping her flippers together in a gesture of willingness.

With Dolphin on the team, Eagle turned his attention elsewhere. "And now," he said, "for the Soil Dwellers." Eagle peered toward the edge of the forest and focused on the one place everyone else seemed to overlook: the Great Ant Hill, where a colony of ants continued to work furiously in spite of the hustle and bustle around them. "Excuse me, ants?" said Eagle, politely interrupting their work.

The Colony continued to pass along the food from one to another until one heroic-looking ant among them held up a hand, bringing the others to an abrupt pause. He looked up at Eagle, and the others followed his lead.

"The Colony," said Eagle, "has had a hand in more accomplishments than the rest of us combined. Can we count on all of you to help?"

"You can always count on us!" said Ant, proudly. "We'll work harder than ever before, too, if it means we *all* benefit."

The rest of the Colony cheered, raised their arms, and jumped around in support while Ant smiled confidently.

Eagle nodded with assurance, "Absolutely, for the good of us *all*."

Chameleon emerged from the shrub where she had landed earlier and nodded along with Eagle. "I agree," she consented, to no one's surprise.

Yet not all of the animals were in agreement, and the more Bear pondered it the more upset he got. He felt threatened, and realized he was losing control. It was easy

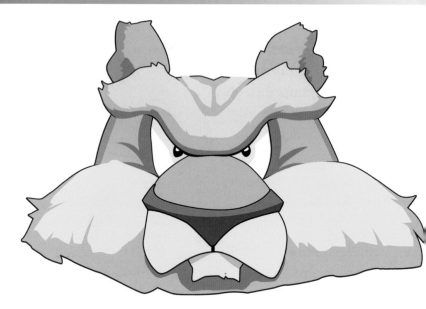

to see in his glaring eyes that his hurt had given seed to anger, and that future resistance had taken root in the present.

THE VISION EMERGES

Eagle knew that pulling together the right team was one of the most important things he himself could do. But now it was time for *teamwork*. So the newly formed Coalition began by observing the other animals around them. They listened to what each animal had to say—learning how the Great Change would affect them—and sought to understand their individual thoughts, feelings, and needs for survival.

Gathering the right teams to get the *correct and complete* information the Coalition needed finally paid off. Some efforts were more successful than others, but it was never easy. Yet no matter to whom they spoke or how they were welcomed, one constant remained: almost everyone had hope. It was hope for *a land blooming with opportunity for all,* and that was a start.

Soon the Coalition began to realize that this hope was actually the start of something huge! It was bigger than each of them as individuals, bigger than the team, and possibly bigger than anything they had seen before. That spark of hope for *a land blooming with opportunity for all* ignited a vision for the good of everyone who lived in Oldland. And that vision spread its flames the moment members of the Ant Colony raised their fists and united a team against the hidden fears of dying hope.

"Keep . . . hope . . . alive," said Ant. "Keep hope alive. Keep hope alive! *Keep hope alive!*"

Soon Owl, Dolphin, and Lion joined in with the Colony. "Keep hope alive! Keep hope alive!" they all cheered.

Eagle smiled and finally began to believe that they might survive after all. "Keep hope alive!" he shouted, joining in the cheer, and a vision of *a land blooming with opportunity for all* was born.

RESISTANCE BEGINS

Later, back at the Meeting Place, the animals gathered once more to hear what the Coalition had to report. Not all of them were happy to be there.

"What is it *now*?" screamed Bear. "You want us to listen to more of your crazy ideas?"

Eagle ignored Bear's remarks and addressed the animals. "My friends," he said, "in the past few weeks, the team and I have been talking to you about the Great Change. We've taken all your ideas and concerns and used them to create a vision. Thanks to you, we finally know what must be done."

With great sadness, Eagle shared with the animals what the team had learned about the effects of the Great Change. He told them how Resource River was fading away and how Nostalgia Desert was gaining ground every day. He did not, however, speak alone.

Owl wisely had observed that the recent rains that should have helped only made things worse. Rain had brought lightning, and lightning had sparked the dry vegetation—causing a reign of fire and devastation.

With a weary sigh, Owl warned everyone that satisfying immediate needs and embracing temporary solutions only drains the land's resources more quickly. She told them how Resource River was drying up from everyone's shortsighted actions. If this continued, Resource River would soon be nothing but a murky, puddled riverbed drained of its once great capability to sustain them all.

Ant also piped up. Backed by members of the Colony, he offered perhaps the most chilling observation of all. He noted that by trying to survive individually, the animals were drifting further and further apart, and that by focusing on the parts, they were breaking up the whole. This was something the Colony could not understand.

"Everyone!" Ant shouted for attention. "You've got to listen to me! We've got to let go of old *assumptions*, denial, and negativity, or we'll never find a solution! Look," he continued more calmly, "all that the Colony knows for sure is we've got to find a new home. Oldland just can't support us anymore!"

"Ha!" interrupted Bear. "A new land? You mean a land of opportunity for Eagle and his team! How about the rest of us?"

"I agree!" yelled Chameleon.

"Yeah, yeah," added Hyena sarcastically. "We've heard it all before, Eagle! Ooooh, the Great Change! What a load of guano! As if change ever worked or ever will!"

"I agree!" Chameleon said once again with a nod.

A smooth yet arrogant voice was suddenly heard over the dissident noise. "Citizens! Pleassse calm yourselvesss," hissed Snake as he slithered his way to the front of the group.

"What's all the fuss? Things aren't *that* bad," he subtly continued. "Everyone just needs to sssettle down a little.

"You know," said Snake, "I've sssseen it all—from the land to the trees to the sssoil to the water—and I can tell you, we are all different. Not one of us is the sssame. But I must sssay it's so good to open up to each other like thisss, don't you think? Even if all this talk of a new land is nothing but a sssad illusion."

Snake smiled broadly in his sly way, and Eagle felt the animals' focus begin to wane. "You're wrong. This is not an illusion!" asserted Eagle. "Grain by grain, the sand of Nostalgia Desert has crept into our world. If we don't pull together to find a new home, it will smother us all!"

SEEKING A STRATEGY

Snake's clever words spread like poison, and he blinded the other animals to the truth with his lies. But there can be a kernel of truth in every untruth. Snake was right about one thing: they were all different. However, it was these differences—their backgrounds, talents, and perspectives—that were their greatest treasure.

So the Coalition gathered near the waterfall deep within the jungle to listen closely to one another and learn. Because their survival and success were linked to their ability to communicate with each other first, they chose to hear each member's opinion and gain each individual's unique point of view, even if these were different from their own.

Owl explained the need to nest deeper in the forest, while Lion shared his challenges of finding food and water. Ant and the Colony spelled out the difficulties of digging through the brittle earth, and Dolphin begged to be free of the crowded, shallow waters. And Eagle described the thick, hot air and the alarming scene from up above.

Listening to one another's unique needs only strengthened their commitment to find a solution to lead the other inhabitants to a new land. Owl cautioned the team that leading the animals might require sacrifice. So they were all prepared to do what was necessary to find a new land blooming with opportunity for all.

Eagle remained especially focused. And although resistance was growing, he never wavered from his goal or weakened in his resolve. When a small group of trusted Air Dwellers was sent to survey the borders of the region in search of options, Eagle took wing and joined them in their quest. But this challenge wasn't just about finding a new land blooming with opportunity for all. It was about holding on to hope for survival. So Eagle had a plan for spreading hope throughout the land, and this plan involved the Grapevine.

The Grapevine had always been a center of activity, where busybody bees whispered gossip and spread it throughout the land. Eagle knew that whoever won control of the Grapevine could win the minds of the animals. He also knew that the Resistance had recruited Busy Bee to spread negative ideas through the Grapevine. That is why Eagle needed a powerful and popular hero to take the sting out of Bee's network while he was away searching for a new land. So Eagle recruited Ant.

Ant made his way to the Grapevine to search for Busy Bee—the self-proclaimed ruler of the

Grapevine. It did not take long for him to find Bee. He was at the center of the activity, humming to himself with a smug look of self-importance.

Ant dropped down from a vine above and quietly made his way toward Bee, until he paused right behind Bee.

"Ahhhhhhhhhhh!" screamed Bee, startled by Ant as he darted straight up in the air and fluttered down again. "*Ant!* Man, you scared me half to death!"

"Did I?" said Ant innocently. "Sorry. I'm just here to use the Grapevine."

"Oh, yeah?" asked Bee suspiciously. "What for?"

"We need to have a gathering right away," said Ant. "Eagle says . . ."

"Whoa ho ho ho!" interrupted Bee. "Well, if Eagle says . . . I don't think so!"

"Are you really that blind?" asked Ant in disbelief. "A common vision is right in front of you!"

Bee stared silently at Ant and rolled his eyes

skyward, but Ant continued in vain to inject some common sense.

"You could be so much more than just a tool for gossip," said Ant. "You could be a major voice here!"

"I've got news for you, hero," replied Bee while sticking a finger into Ant's chest. "I already am. I run this Grapevine."

Ant's eyes narrowed in determination as he made a bold prediction. "Not anymore!" he said defiantly.

Seeing Ant's resolve, Bee nervously backed away and quickly flew off, fearing a confrontation. Ant was now free to address the other bees that had gathered during the exchange.

"Bees! Listen to me!" he boldly announced. "We are all in terrible danger and there is so little time. Even as we speak, Nostalgia Desert is creeping closer, making its way here to the Grapevine," he said pointing. "But don't give up hope. The Air Dwellers are searching for a new haven. Now, *go*, quickly! We meet here again tonight!"

All the bees quickly dashed off in different directions to spread the word of the gathering, and Ant looked off in the distance after them. Communication lines had been opened, and Ant was proud of the role he had played. Now, he hoped the Air Dwellers would be equally successful.

THE PLAN

That night, the animals met by the light of a full moon to share what they had learned. Eagle, once again standing upon the central stump at the Meeting Place, was bursting with the news that the Air Dwellers' mission was a success!

"We've found it!" Eagle cried. "Our new home. But," he cautioned, "for many of you, it won't be easy to get there."

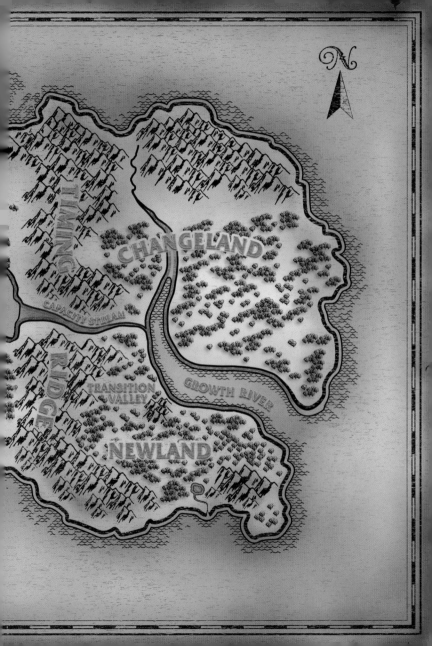

Truer words were never spoken. To reach the new land, the animals would need somehow to cross Transition Valley and treacherous regions where water and other resources would be scarce—but hope was not entirely lost. There was a source of water: sluggish, narrow Capacity Stream, which meandered from its source at Leverage Lake through Timing Ridge and into Growth River in the new land. It was clear to all that the success of such a journey would likely rest on the amount of water flowing from Leverage Lake into Capacity Stream at the junction on Timing Ridge.

It was a lot to risk on something so uncertain, but Eagle and the team felt that there was no other option. If they succeeded, the rewards would be worth the effort, but that didn't make it any easier to reach a decision about what to do and how to do it.

And so the dialogue continued throughout the night . . . until the first rays of dawn finally brought clarity.

THE PLAN
MADE WHOLE

By morning, some of the animals had left the Meeting Place, but most remained. Many of the animals slept in nervous slumber, others lay exhausted, and the rest continued to think. Rabbit was a thinker. He was sitting on the ground drawing in the sand with a stick, but no ideas seemed to take form.

Suddenly inspiration struck, and Rabbit had a brilliant idea. At least he thought it was brilliant, and he had come to a point where he could think out loud with the group.

"Hey! Hey! I've got it!" he said.

Quickly sketching in the sand, Rabbit began to formulate his idea. "Okay. We're gonna need a big tree . . . then we build this thingy here," he said, talking to himself. "Get a really huge animal to test it—couple of tons." (Hippo gulped in protest.) "Hmmm. Better get a bigger tree." Rabbit continued his outspoken thoughts as a shadow formed behind him.

When he was finished, Rabbit had drawn a large but crude looking catapult designed to launch animals from Comfort Valley, over Timing Ridge, and into the new land. "Umm . . . on second thought, it would never work," he proclaimed. "A project of this magnitude . . . you gotta have perfect timing, maximum capacity, and all that leverage. It'll never happen."

Lion had watched and listened as he stood behind Rabbit, inspecting the crude drawing. He raised an eyebrow and asked, "Did you just say timing . . . leverage . . . capacity? Hmmm," Lion said, raising a claw to scratch his chin. "You know what? It might just work!"

"Hey, everybody," shouted Lion, "Rabbit just gave us a great idea!"

"I did?" said Rabbit, looking bewildered. "I mean . . . I did. Of course, I did," said Rabbit, correcting himself.

The other animals began to gather around Rabbit and Lion, and listened as Lion explained. While Rabbit's idea was not the solution, it did light the fire of invention and served as a stepping-stone to formulate a plan. Lion had added his thoughts and plans to Rabbit's idea, but he was careful not to take credit for Rabbit's original idea so that he would continue to get more new ideas from Rabbit and the others. Bold and daring, Lion's plan would take a lot of teamwork and effort to pull off.

The plan was to dig a canal through Comfort Valley from Resource River to Leverage Lake. By diverting water from Resource River to Leverage Lake, the animals could create an overflow that would supply more water to Capacity Stream—increasing its capability to carry more water through Transition Valley to Growth River in the new land. There was danger in the very real possibility that they might miscalculate and lose all the water from Resource River before their arrival in the new land—but they had to try.

With growing interest from the animals, Lion took action. He began by recruiting Wolf to begin the process. Working as a lone wolf and also with various teams, Wolf could lead his pack through Transition Valley—researching and developing areas along the way. Wolf knew that this path would be long and treacherous, so he suggested interludes of short-term rest and special rewards.

Next, Beaver was asked to lead the effort to divert Resource River into Leverage Lake as well as to places of relaxation and celebration along

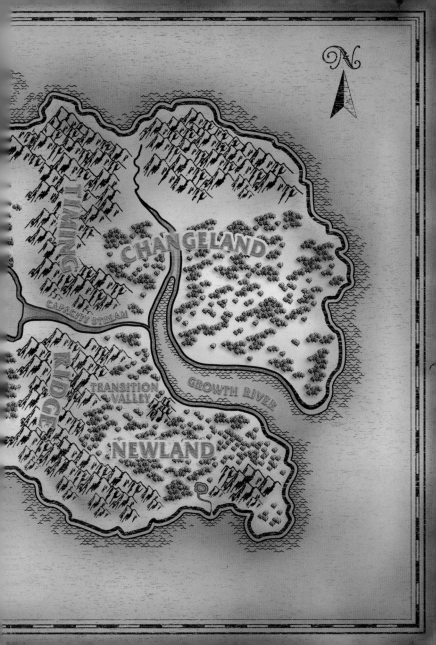

Transition Valley to let the animals taste the fruits of their success. Cheetah was chosen to quickly, accurately, and thoroughly coordinate the information flow back and forth from the Coalition to the front lines. Finally, Lion convinced Ant, Dolphin, and Owl that they would be needed to ensure success.

Ant and the Colony would recruit other Soil Dwellers and Dolphin would coordinate the Water Dwellers. Owl, meanwhile, would direct the animals that lived south of the new course for Resource River to make their way to Leverage Lake. It was a good plan, but resistance remained.

THE RESISTANCE

While Lion was explaining the plan and the animals joined in excited discussion, nobody noticed a shadowy figure approaching from behind Lion and Rabbit.

"Sssssooo," hissed Snake, sneakily emerging from behind Rabbit, "you think we're just going to let you dessstroy Comfort Valley—our home—with this insssane plan? If you fail," he shouted, "we all die! Persssonally, I think we should leave everything as it isss! We don't need to do thisss!"

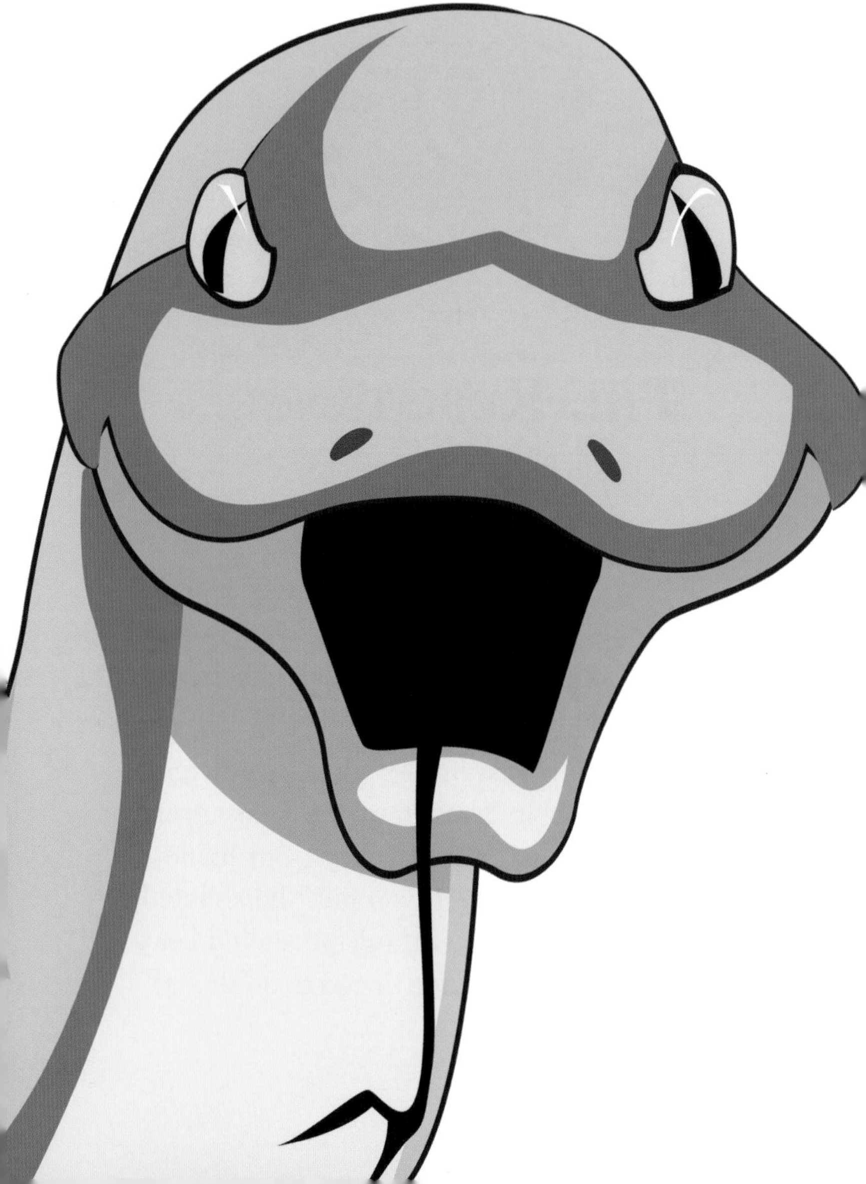

"No!" cried Eagle.

All eyes turned to see Eagle, who had silently joined the group. "You may shed your skin, but you're always the same old Snake," said Eagle to Snake. "If you were resisting the Great Change for a reason—pride, past betrayals, confusion—I could understand. But you . . . *you* do it because it's simply your nature. No excuses."

Snake raised himself to his maximum height and looked defiantly into the eyes of Eagle. "You won't sssucceed," challenged Snake. "I won't let you!"

"*You,*" said Eagle with emphasis, "have nothing to do with *our* success."

"We shall sssee," hissed Snake, as his eyes narrowed. Then, as suddenly has he had appeared, Snake slithered off into the jungle.

THE DINOSAUR GRAVEYARD

Snake's brazen resistance brought a cloud of darkness over Eagle—although he did not let anyone see the depth of his concern. As the daylight moved toward dusk, Eagle took flight and landed at the site of the mysterious Dinosaur Graveyard.

As the darkness began to settle in, Eagle sat on an old tree branch looking out among the

fossilized bones of the ancient animals—some partially covered by plant life and others embedded in the rocks. He sat and he thought . . . and thought . . . and thought. But nothing he thought about seemed to ease his mind or erase his concerns.

    With grace, Owl lighted on the branch next to Eagle. She was worried about her friend and had been searching for him. But noticing Eagle's grim look, she decided to sit quietly by her friend's side and not interrupt his pondering.

Eagle finally broke the cold silence. "I've been coming here a lot lately," said Eagle, not looking at Owl. "We're not going to make it, are we?"

Owl looked up at Eagle, smiling like a mother hen and partially amused by his last statement. "Now why would you say a thing like that?" she asked.

Eagle pointed out to the graveyard—toward a rather large set of dinosaur bones. "They didn't survive," he said, "and look how much bigger they were."

Eagle looked down at Owl and was met with a reassuring smile. "They just couldn't deal with change," she offered, "and if you're not *leading* change . . . you're history."

"You're right," Eagle sighed. "I just wish I knew that what I'm doing is right." He looked off into the distance once more, unsure of what to do next.

"I feel like we are doing the right thing in order to survive," said Owl. "I'm sure some of us won't make it—just like these dinosaurs." Owl gave a wave of her wing. "Old friends may say goodbye forever," she added with sorrow. "Others will fade away. But, I *believe* in you."

Then, with a gleam of hope in her face, Owl offered the light Eagle was seeking. "You've got to focus on those who see the vision of Newland . . . and make it happen," she said. "Remember: keep hope alive, and nothing will keep you from Newland."

Eagle, raising his brow in confusion, said, "Newland?"

"Can you think of a better name?" replied Owl.

"No," said Eagle. "I like it."

And with that, Eagle and Owl both

looked off into the distance as the last light of the sun dipped into the darkness. They knew that tomorrow marked a new day, and the beginning of their journey to Newland.

THE JOURNEY

Thus the journey began, and all the animals knew that life would never be the same. Wolf and his pack got an early start scouting the lands surrounding Timing Ridge. They began to identify the best paths and marked areas where the animals could rest. With the help of the beavers, Wolf was able to inform the Coalition as to where Resource River could be diverted to feed small basins intended to sustain the animals on their journey. It was important, as Wolf had earlier surmised, to plan for areas of rest and celebration of their small successes along Transition Valley.

Cheetah proved herself by racing from one group to another—listening intently before speaking. She was fast and accurate, and her communication was *correct and complete*—allowing the Coalition to stay in touch with the different groups of animals working to make the plan a reality.

Beaver utilized the strength of Elephant, Rhino, and Hippo to form dams using all the natural resources at their disposal. Soon Air Dwellers were dropping useful sticks, vines, and rocks for the beavers' needs. It wasn't long before the beavers began to solidify the many dams necessary to divert Resource River and control its flow.

Rabbit and the many Soil Dwellers dug tirelessly to carve a trench from Resource River to Leverage Lake. Snake, Bear, and the other resistors scoffed at their efforts—declaring it was impossible to accomplish what they had set out to do. This only caused the animals to work harder than before, and soon a canal began to take form.

For weeks the inhabitants worked diligently together and made amazing progress, even overcoming the threatening tactics of the Resistance. But through it all, Eagle and the Coalition not only led the animals' efforts to succeed but also worked to ensure that the vision was never lost.

Finally, the water from Resource River had been diverted and was being held in check by a great dam formed from the contributions of the different inhabitants. A canal between the dam and Leverage Lake waited for its time to carry water to Leverage Lake, and a widened Capacity Stream stood ready to accept the eventual overflow.

All was going according to the plan, but the animals were exhausted. They celebrated their success briefly, chanting "Keep hope alive!" in unison and congratulating one another on their efforts. Then they rested—waiting for the proper time to direct Resource River toward the leverage point at Timing Ridge.

TIME FOR TRANSITION

When Eagle gave the signal, the animals watched in awe as the water gushed down the canal and into Leverage Lake. Then when the timing was right, Beaver caused the final dam to fall, and the rushing waters from Resource River flowed freely into the widened Capacity Stream.

Snake, who had never believed this was possible and who was looking for any way to spoil

the animals' efforts, was swept away in the surging flood—never to be seen again.

The animals cheered in unison at what they had accomplished. The plan had worked. Now they were ready to complete their journey. So they continued their trek along Capacity Stream through Transition Valley.

They had never anticipated Transition Valley to be so treacherous, and many challenging changes had happened at this juncture in the blink of an eye—the damburst, Snake's demise, and Capacity Stream suddenly flowing wide and deep.

Owl had warned that after so many speedy victories the animals might slow their pace and lose focus. Wolf had also warned that Transition Valley could be daunting, so Eagle planned a special time of celebration and rest at one of the basins that Wolf and Beaver had prepared in advance.

As dusk arrived, the silhouettes of the animals could be seen in front of the canopy of colors on the horizon as they walked wearily but happily to their place of celebration and rest. Eagle planned to meet the next day with all the animals one last time before stepping out of Transition Valley into Newland. Little did he know what would happen the next morning as the animals gathered. . . .

CONFLICT ARISES

The next morning, as they gathered beneath a glorious sunrise sky, Eagle began his meeting with all the animals.

"Well, we're almost there!" he said. "Let's rest here while Cheetah runs ahead with some of the Air Dwellers to make sure everything is safe."

"Hold on, Flyboy!" shouted Bear, angrily waving his fist. "Who put you and your *coalition* in charge? And how come you get to decide who goes into Newland first?"

"Yeah!" stormed Shark, angrily rising out of the water of Capacity Stream. "We all worked hard to get here! I thought this was supposed to be a land of opportunity for *all*! Maybe I wanna go first!"

A breeze of uneasiness began to blow as the animals started to join in with cries of "*Yes*" and "*I agree.*"

Turtle timidly suggested, "We could draw straws."

Turtle's idea was met with much grumbling and a resounding "*No!*" So Turtle withdrew her

head into her shell, and the whites of her eyes blinked in the darkness.

The winds of conflict had arrived, but Dolphin was not about to let them destroy everything after they had come so far together. She rose out of the water, higher than Shark, and tried to be a soothing force. "Everybody just calm down," she said assertively. "Look, we're so close . . . don't ruin it now! There's got to be some kind of solution where everybody wins."

Fox thought for a moment and offered a suggestion. "Okay, let's see," she said. "Um . . . yeah . . . I know . . . we could all take turns going first! That way, nobody's first all the time and nobody's last all the time."

Nobody really embraced the idea, so Owl quickly spoke up as a storm of grumbles began to brew once more. "Wait! I think I may have a third option in which everybody wins," she offered. "How about if each group selects someone to represent them? That way, a representative from each group could enter the valley—at the same time."

Many of the animals looked to one another, each considering the third option suggested by Owl.

"Don't you see?"

Owl said. "In a way, everyone goes first and no one really goes last. And the representatives can choose the land that best suits their group's needs."

Now convinced, the animals all raised their voices in agreement with a celebratory "*Yaaaayyy!*"

Eagle, now standing next to Owl, placed a wing on her shoulder and looked down. "My dear friend," he said, "what would we do without your wisdom? Valuing our differences is always a winning solution."

Owl smiled broadly, and just as their differences, backgrounds, talents, and perspectives had formed the initial vision and strategy, they also delivered them safely to their new home.

FINALLY HOME

The animals made their way along the sparkling waters of Growth River as they followed its lush and bountiful banks through a thick field of vegetation. When they finally emerged from the jungle, they were met with the sight of a gorgeous hidden valley: Newland, blooming in all of its glory.

The animals stared in awe at the richness of plants, the abundance of water, and the vast

mountains. It was far beyond their wildest expectations. Nothing, however, is perfect. Sometimes the terrain was difficult to navigate, and the currents of Growth River could be wild and unpredictable, but this new land was fertile and

blossomed with more opportunity than they had ever experienced before.

Once they settled in, the members of the Coalition took time to coach those who would eventually replace them so that future generations

would be prepared to face similar challenges. This wasn't easy, because it's hard to prepare for the future when you're enjoying the present, and it took a long time for those who hadn't actually experienced the Great Change to embrace the

lessons from the difficult transition. Yet this was a task that was too important to ignore, and they made it a priority.

Some of those who had resisted in the past actually began to believe. Hyena actually began to smile—not that she would let anyone catch her smiling.

And so the animals learned to make change a permanent part of their lives in Newland. They discovered new ways of thinking, and the more they discovered, the more ways they invented to make life better. Life would never be the same.

LESSONS LEARNED

One day, Eagle and Owl sat on a branch overlooking Newland. Eagle was deep in thought as he stared off into the valley. He didn't even notice Chameleon climbing onto the branch to sit next to him.

"What are you thinking about?" asked Owl.

"The ones we left behind," replied Eagle, "and the opportunity they all lost."

"Poor Snake," said Owl, "he just couldn't let go of Comfort Valley—even as it wilted before his very eyes. I don't think he ever understood why we all wanted to risk the journey and the changing currents of Growth River on the hope of something better."

"We've all learned so much," added Eagle, "about leadership and embracing our differences . . . and change. It's been good for us."

Owl looked up slightly at Eagle. "You know," she said, "change will come again."

"Yes," said Eagle confidently, "but now we'll be ready."

"I agree," said Chameleon, to no one in particular.

Eagle glanced down at Chameleon, surprised that she was there. Her shoulders shrugged and she grinned up at Eagle, blushing slightly.

Then, with a pause and a quick smile, Eagle quickly tipped her off the tree branch, and she tumbled once again into the shrubs below. Eagle and Owl laughed as a puff of leaves from Chameleon's landing caught wind and took flight. Whether it was the wind of change that carried the leaves out into the valley or not, it did not matter.

The inhabitants of Newland had learned the lessons of leadership by experiencing the possibilities of vision, the paradox of diverse consensus, the power of collective respect and trust, the magic of active listening and dialogue, and the beauty of the third option. They learned the secrets of sharing values while valuing their differences and leading transformational change to create a better world. They were now ready for Newland and beyond.

About the Author

Bill Poole is CEO and president of LifeLead International, based in Tampa, Florida. An international author, speaker, coach, and consultant, he is an innovative pioneer in personal, team, and organizational capability.

Bill leads a worldwide network of LifeLead associates who serve as facilitators, coaches, and consultants and who share the vision of "building lives and leaders."

His work with successful international training organizations; large organizations such as Coca-Cola, Nike, IBM, Caterpillar, and Wachovia; and small and medium-sized organizations in transition provides a solid foundation for his collaborative partnerships and creative processes for transformational change.

Bill's practical expertise provides the basis for the *Journey to Newland: A Road Map for Transformational Change* storybook and movie. He is also a coproducer of the animated movie and the coauthor and collaborator for all *Journey to Newland* courses and games, which are enjoyed throughout the world in many languages.

Bill's business experience and educational background in communication, psychology, philosophy, and religion provide relevant insights toward producing innovative processes with creative teaching approaches.

Bill lives in Tampa, Florida, and can be contacted at bpoole@lifeleadint.com.

ABOUT THE COLLABORATORS

Daryl Holt is the former vice president of Paper 2 Pixel Creative Group in Orlando, Florida, and is a key contributor and creative consultant for many *Journey to Newland*–related projects. As the primary author of the *Journey to Newland* screenplay, Daryl was instrumental in translating the dialogue and images from the animated production of *Journey to Newland* to the storybook format you see here. He also codirected the animated movie with Jason Renfroe.

Daryl currently lives in Orlando, Florida, where he is the central creative development director at Electronic Arts—Tiburon. Daryl also continues to offer his strategic and creative expertise on many business, entertainment, and marketing projects nationwide.

Andy Dorsett is a professional illustrator whose work appears in a variety of print and multimedia formats. As the lead character designer on the animated version of *Journey to Newland,* Andy developed the interpretation of the characters that has served as a lynchpin for *Journey to Newland* and related projects.

Andy, a graduate of the Ringling School of Art and Design, currently lives in Tampa, Florida. He provides illustrations and artwork for the *Tampa Tribune* newspaper and utilizes his eighteen years of professional illustration experience to bring creative vision to many freelance projects.